MW01088649

ENTRY AND EXIT CONFESSIONS OF A CHAMPION TRADER

52 Ways a Professional Speculator Gets In and Out of the Stock, Futures and Forex Markets

Kevin J. Davey

Kevin J. Davey

ISBN: 9781095328552 (paperback)

Printed in the United States of America

First Printing: April 2019

Visit my website at KJTradingsystems.com

Table of Contents

DISCLAIMER

Data, information, and material ("content") is provided for informational and educational purposes only. This material neither is, nor should be construed as an offer, solicitation, or recommendation to buy or sell any securities. Any investment decisions made by the user through the use of such content is solely based on the users independent analysis taking into consideration your financial circumstances, investment objectives, and risk tolerance. Neither KJTradingSystems.com (KJ Trading) nor any of its content providers shall be liable for any errors or for any actions taken in reliance thereon. By accessing the KJ Trading site, a user agrees not to redistribute the content found therein unless specifically authorized to do so.

Individual performance depends upon each student's unique skills, time commitment, and effort. Results may not be typical and individual results will vary.

U.S. Government Required Disclaimer - Commodity Futures Trading Commission states: Futures and Options trading has large potential rewards, but also large potential risk. You must be aware of the risks and be willing to accept them in order to invest in the futures and options markets. Don't trade with money you can't afford to lose. This is neither a solicitation nor an offer to Buy/Sell futures, stocks or options on the same. No representation is being made that any account will or is likely to achieve profits or losses similar to those discussed in this document. The past performance of any trading system or methodology is not necessarily indicative of future results.

CFTC RULE 4.41 - HYPOTHETICAL OR SIMULATED PERFORMANCE RESULTS HAVE CERTAIN LIMITATIONS. UNLIKE AN ACTUAL PERFORMANCE RECORD, SIMULATED RESULTS DO NOT REPRESENT ACTUAL TRADING. ALSO, SINCE THE TRADES HAVE NOT BEEN EXECUTED, THE RESULTS MAY HAVE UNDER-OR-OVER COMPENSATED FOR THE IMPACT, IF ANY, OF CERTAIN MARKET FACTORS, SUCH AS LACK OF LIQUIDITY. SIMULATED

TRADING PROGRAMS IN GENERAL ARE ALSO SUBJECT TO THE FACT THAT THEY ARE DESIGNED WITH THE BENEFIT OF HINDSIGHT. NO REPRESENTATION IS BEING MADE THAT ANY ACCOUNT WILL OR IS LIKELY TO ACHIEVE PROFIT OR LOSSES SIMILAR TO THOSE SHOWN.

NO REPRESENTATION IS BEING MADE THAT ANY ACCOUNT WILL, OR IS LIKELY TO ACHIEVE PROFITS OR LOSSES SIMILAR TO THOSE DISCUSSED WITHIN THIS SITE. IF YOU DECIDE TO INVEST REAL MONEY, ALL TRADING DECISIONS SHOULD BE YOUR OWN.

GRAB MY BONUS MATERIAL

Before you begin, simply go to http://www.AOKbooks.com/52book to get these bonuses:

·   **"6 Nifty Extras"** – not entries, not exits, but instead useful code snippets for Tradestation you can use
·   **44 minute video "3 Excellent Entries"** – advanced entry techniques, not discussed here
·   **"9 Terrific Trading Entries, 7 Sensible Exits"** free e-book – new entries/exits not in this book
·   **Invitations to free trading webinars** I regularly put on, and podcasts where I discuss trading
·   **All entries and exits discussed in the book**, in Tradestation format as ELD files, ready to import.

THANKS!

INTRODUCTION

I love trading. Stocks, futures, forex – I love trading them all. I have enjoyed trading ever since that first day I received a direct mail piece at my apartment, extolling the virtues of speculating in the sugar futures market.

I love uncovering trading ideas, modifying them and turning them into trading strategies. I create "algos" – trading strategy algorithms that make the buy and sell decisions for me. I also automate most of them, which keeps me from interfering!

Using algos I created, I was able to finish in 1st or 2nd place three different years in a worldwide, real money, year-long futures trading contest. In each of those years, I was able to achieve over 100% annual return. Hence my moniker "Champion Trader."

I have also taught or consulted with many other trading contest winners, including the contest winners in 2017 and 2018. So the algos I use work for me, and I have been able to teach the process I use so others can be successful, too.

There is a great thrill in developing a trading strategy, testing it over history to see how profitable it has been, and then running it with real money on the line – especially if it makes money.

That is what I do, day in and day out. It is algo trading in a nutshell – you take some entries and exits, combine them into a strategy, then test and evaluate the strategy on historical data. If it is profitable, and meets all your criteria, you then turn the algo loose on a market or markets. If things work out right (and they don't always work out right, trust me on that), you should be able to earn a reasonable risk adjusted rate of return.

The process to properly develop an algo is complicated – it is not as simple as applying the strategy to a chart and optimizing like crazy– and is advanced material not included in this book. But any algo has to start with the basic components: entries and exits.

That is what this book is all about, getting you started with developing trading algos. In the sections that follow, you'll notice that I tend to keep things simple. I don't have (or recommend) entries with 10 or 20 conditions, rules or filters just to get a buy or sell signal.

My experience is that overly complicated strategies are just too much. Based on 25+ years of trading, I can tell you that the market tends to agree with me – simple usually works best.

What is interesting is I like keeping not just the idea simple, but the code simple, too. I can't always do that, though. I do have some simple ideas, but the code is pretty complicated. Don't worry, though - I did not include them in this book.

In this book, you will find 41 unique entries, and 11 exits. These are all used by me in at least one, and sometimes multiple, strategies I personally trade now, have traded in the past, or have extensively tested and evaluated. So, they have been battle tested, with most proven to work with real money. But don't take my word for it – TEST THESE YOURSELF!

Not every entry works in every market, nor with every bar size. The same hold true with exits. But the entries and exits I provide can, and do, work in quite a few situations.

NOTE: Although I am primarily a futures trader, the entries and exits in this book also apply to stocks, CFDS, forex, etc. You just have to test them in those markets.

So, with that, let's get started!

WHAT THIS BOOK IS NOT

If you've bought this book expecting to have ready-made strategies provided that you can immediately trade with zero effort on your part, I suggest you just return the book right now.

This book is not intended to spoon feed you trading strategies. Why not?

Well, first, if I did provide complete strategies, with defined markets, timeframes, parameters and everything you need to get started, for strategies that actually work in the real world, you would have to pay a lot more money than what you did for this book! No successful active trader I know of will give away profitable, complete strategies for free or miniscule cost. Keep that in mind as you are bombarded by trading educators on the Internet, offering free or "secret" strategies for minimal cost.

Second, published strategies tend to degrade after publication. Whether this is just normal strategy lifecycle degradation, or maybe because many traders suddenly begin trading the published strategy – thereby taking away the edge - I don't know. Probably a bit of both. But any full strategies in the public domain are not likely to remain high performers for too long.

Finally, just giving you strategies goes against my philosophy, which is: "Give a man a fish, and he eats for a day. Teach him how to fish, and he can eat everyday."

An example: I have a friend who wanted his son to get into a specific university so badly that he (the father) wrote the application essays for the son. How is that good - for the father, the son or the school? It isn't!

Rather than just feeding traders some fish, I try to teach them how to fish for themselves. That is what this book does – it teaches you, and really provides a lot of bait and equipment so you can start to create strategies (successfully fish) on your own.

I expect you to test the ideas in this book, put them together, modify them, etc. In other words, use them to improve your algo trading skills and strategy building abilities. This will give you confidence in your trading, which is awesome (and necessary) if you want to be a self-sufficient trader.

Oh, by the way, my friend's son had his application denied. Not sure if either of them learned a lesson, though.

HOW THIS BOOK IS STRUCTURED

I have created a separate chapter for each entry, and for each exit. For all the entries and exits, you will typically see:

- **A short explanation of the concept.** I believe the best entries and exits should have some logical reasoning behind it. This is where I differ from machine learning purists. A machine learning program can say "when close of 13 bars ago is greater than the close of 47 bars ago, buy" and maybe that strategy does well historically. But, is there any relevance behind the close of 13 and 47 bars ago, or is just a random "blind squirrel eventually finds a nut" situation? Machine learning is great at finding profitable relationships, but many are spurious – meaning they are just fluke situations. I favor entries and exits that I can reasonably explain and understand.

- **The code in Tradestation (Easy Language) format.** If you use Multicharts, the code should work for that platform, too. You will have to translate either my plain English description, or the Easy Language code, to get it in your favorite trading platform. I should mention that Easy Language is called that for a reason! It is my trading strategy programming language of choice, and I think you should consider it if you want to program strategies quickly.

- **Plain English Code.** Many of you probably do not use Tradestation, so I have also included simple rules in plain English. You should be able to take what I have written, and code it in the programming language of your choice. Some features and functions I use which are available in Tradestation may not be available in your software platform. So, you might have to do some additional programming for some of the entries and exits.

- **Example Charts.** For some of the entries, I include a sample equity curve for that entry, with a simple exit added in. My intent with this book is not to give you full strategies, but rather good pieces for you to build your own strategies with. So, these sample equity charts give you an idea of what is possible, but it is up to you to get to that point.

NOTE: For all the entries and exits I provide, I do NOT claim to be the original creator of any of these ideas – although I may have been. These ideas may have come from a book I read, a magazine article, the Internet, or I may have just dreamt them up. For most of them, I have no idea (no pun intended) where they came from. Typically, I find ideas out there, and then immediately modify them to my liking. Chances are that is the case with many of these entries and exits. I have tried to give credit where I know the original author.

SUGGESTED PLAN OF ATTACK

Even though this is a short book, the information provided in it could literally keep you busy developing strategies for years. It can be overwhelming. So, here is what I recommend:

1. Read through the book from beginning to end. Don't spend a lot of time examining the entries and exits – there will be plenty of time for that later – but get through all the sections. That will give you a good foundation for future work.

2. Have a defined plan for how you are going to test each entry and exit. That plan should include the markets you are going to test, the bar sizes (30 minute? 60 minute? Daily?) you want to examine, and most importantly HOW you are going to test the strategies you create. I discuss the proven process I use in a later chapter. You should use a testing process that you know works (meaning, one that produces strategies that deliver real money profits). Just optimizing is not going to work!

3. Since there are 52 entries and exits, you could select one each week for a year. For example, in the first week, take Entry #1, add in an exit or two, and start to test markets with it. As you progress during the week, you might think of filters to add to the entry, or simplifications/modifications to the code I give you.

In week 2, simply move on to Entry #2, and continue this approach every week throughout the year. That will mean this book will last you a year!

Or, maybe if you have the time, you can evaluate 2 entries/exits per week. The key is not to spend too much time on any entry or exit. Touch them lightly, I always tell my Strategy Factory® students. It is easy to test and test until an entry finally gives good results (I call it "testing success by torture"). But usually, the end result is just a curve-fit, over-optimized piece of garbage.

4. Don't forget about the reverse signals. Take the entries I provide, and reverse the buy and sell short signals. That will effectively double the number of entries to test!

5. Don't get discouraged. Most of the tests you run will result in failure, even for the proven entries and exits in this book. They do not work for all markets, and are definitely not universal. Finding good trading strategies, much like trading, is hard work. Certainly much harder than it looks like on Twitter, where no trader/tweeter apparently ever loses!

6. Before you test, make sure your strategy has all of the following components, whether they are from this book or not:
Long entry rule
Short entry rule
Long exit rule
Short exit rule
Position Sizing (if desired, I usually add it in later)
Extras (I provide some nifty little extras in the bonus material available at www.aokbooks.com)

7. Document what you are doing! Keep track of what you test, what works, what doesn't, etc. This helps you see your progress, and also keeps you from repeating tests or analysis.

8. Get going. The only way to create good strategies is to start testing and developing.

OK, now let's get started!

ENTRY #1 – "GO WITH THE FLOW"

General Concept

Two common trading adages are "trade in the direction of momentum" and "cut your losses short." This entry epitomizes both of those.

First, the entry uses a 1 bar momentum – the close of the current bar minus the close of the previous bar. It trades in direction of that very short momentum.

A second condition is as soon as a bar closes with a position showing a loss, the position is reversed.

I have used this entry in the metals sector.

Tradestation Code

Var: openloss(1000); //allowable loss per contract

if close<close[1] and (openpositionprofit<-openloss or marketposition=0) then sellshort next bar at market;
if close>close[1] and (openpositionprofit<-openloss or marketposition=0) then buy next bar at market;

Plain English Code

If the current bar close is less than the previous bar close and if the current position profit is less than negative *openloss* variable or if the current position is flat, sell short at open of next bar.

Do the exact opposite for long positions.

ENTRY #2 – "EVERYONE LOVES FRIDAY"

General Concept

This entry only enters one time per week, at the open Monday (or Sunday night, depending on the market). If the close on Friday is the highest recent close, it will open a long position at the start of the next bar.

When I created this, I believe at the time I was thinking this entry would hold a position over the weekend, since it evaluates each Friday. And maybe that was what I intended. But sometimes, your programming intentions do not match what was actually programmed!

So, this strategy will not enter before a weekend.

Of course, this signal could be made to enter on any day of the week, but I found it worked best for me based on Friday, with a trade on Monday session open.

Note that I use this on daily bars. If you used it on X minute bars, you will have to modify the code to only generate the signal on the last bar of the day.

I have employed this entry in various energies markets.

Tradestation Code

Var:bbars(25); //number of lookback bars for the highest/lowest evaluation

if dayofweek(date)=5 and close=highest(close,bbars) then buy next bar at market;
if dayofweek(date)=5 and close=lowest(close,bbars) then sellshort next bar at market;

Plain English Code

If today is Friday and the close is the highest close of the last *bbars*, then buy at the open of the next bar.

Do the exact opposite for short positions.

ENTRY #3 – "BOOKS CAN BE GREAT"

General Concept

I love reading trading books, since many provide me with new trading ideas. I rarely ever take a strategy I find in a book and trade it as-is, though. I almost always modify the strategy to my liking.

Such is the case with this entry. It comes from the excellent book "Beyond Technical Analysis: How to Develop and Implement a Winning Trading System" by Tushar Chande.

In this case, the strategy Chande describes in his book was a long only entry. I modified it to go long and short.

I have used this entry in stocks and stock indices.

Tradestation Code

Var: shortma(5), longma(10);// short and long moving average lengths

If average(close,shortma) crosses below average(close,longma) and close<average(close,shortma) then buy next bar at market;
If average(close,shortma) crosses above average(close,longma) and close>average(close,shortma) then sellshort next bar at market;

Plain English Code

Calculate 2 moving averages, a short period moving average (with length *shortma*) and a long period moving average (with length *longma*).

If the short moving crosses below the long moving average, and if the close is below the short moving average, then buy the next bar at open.

Do the exact opposite for a short trade.

ENTRY #4 – "BREAKOUT WITH A TWIST"

General Concept

Everyone and their brother has traded or tested a simple breakout approach – buying when new highs are reached. Makes sense, after all. Every up trend is just a series of breakouts to the upside.

The problem is most of the time breakouts fail. I have seen statistics that say 70-80% of breakouts fail, depending on how you define failure. The interesting thing is even with an 80% failure rate, breakouts can still be profitable, if the successful breakouts lead to big trends.

So, to eliminate some of the failed breakouts, this entry uses the ADX indicator as an additional criteria. ADX is supposed to measure the current trendiness of the price – a higher value means a larger trend is in progress.

The entry will only take a signal if the ADX is indicating a non-trending period. This might seem counter intuitive, but the idea is that breakouts during a flat period may be more likely to produce big trends.

I have used this entry in metals.

Tradestation Code

Var: len(10); // length of the lookback period for the breakout

If adx(15)< 20 then Buy next bar at highest(high,len) stop;
If adx(15)< 20 then Sellshort next bar at lowest(low,len) stop;

Plain English Code

Calculate the 15 period ADX indicator. If the current value is below 20, then it is allowable to take a trade.

Buy the next bar at the highest high of the last *len* bars back. Do the exact opposite for a short trade.

Entry #4 with simple stop and profit target

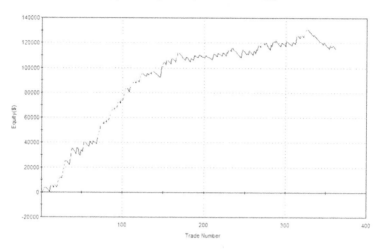

Equity Curve Line - @GC 30 min.(01/02/07 08:30 - 04/10/19 13:00)

ENTRY #5 – "AVERAGE TRUE RANGE BASED BREAKOUT"

General Concept

This entry is fairly similar to Entry #4, since both are breakouts. The difference with this strategy is that the breakout has to be large enough, as measured by the recent average true range, to be triggered. A higher high alone is not enough to go long – it must be a large enough move for the signal to be triggered.

The idea here is that larger moves during a bar are more significant, and those bigger moves help "predict" a higher quality breakout.

I have used this entry in grains and other agricultural markets.

Tradestation Code

Var: XX(1); //multiplier for average true range
Var:ATRval(15); //lookback period for ATR calculation

Buy next bar at close+XX*AvgTrueRange(ATRVal) stop;
Sellshort next bar at close-XX*AvgTrueRange(ATRVal) stop;

Plain English Code

Buy the next bar at the close of the current bar plus the average true range (*ATRval* lookback period) multiplied by factor *XX*. Do the exact opposite for a short trade, except the average true range, multiplied by *XX*, is subtracted from the current bar closing price.

ENTRY #6 – "PERCENT RANKER"

General Concept

This entry is based on the idea that it is better to take short trades when the current close is in the lower range of recent history, and vice versa for long trades. Does it work? Yes, but not in all markets, or at all times (that is why we test!). But the general notion – that low prices lead to lower prices, and high prices lead to higher prices – seems to hold up quite often.

One additional filter that seems to help here is another ADX filter. Trades can only be taken when the ADX indicates a trend, but not a very large trend. This keeps us out during prolonged flat periods, where price might be at top or bottom of a small range.

Tradestation Code

Var: xbars(25); //lookback period for percentile calculation

Value1=percentile(.25,close,xbars); //price at 25th percentile
Value2=percentile(.75,close,xbars); //price at 75th percentile

If ADX(14) >20 AND ADX(14) <30 AND close<Value1 then sellshort next bar at market;
If ADX(14) >20 AND ADX(14) <30 AND close>Value2 then buy next bar at market;

Plain English Code

First, look at the last xbars back. Calculate the 25th percentile of the closing price, assign it to Value1. Calculate the 75th percentile closing price, assign it to Value2.

If the 14 bar ADX value is less than 20 OR greater than 30, no trades can be taken.

If the 14 bar ADX value is less than 30 AND greater than 20, enter short if the current close is less than Value1. Enter long if current close is greater than Value2.

ENTRY #7 – "INTRADAY BREAKOUT"

General Concept

This entry is designed for very short term intraday breakouts. This will not work on daily charts, since there are specific bar times when this pattern can be active.

It is just a simple breakout of highs and lows – you will enter in the direction of the breakout. There is also an ADX filter, so you will be entering only if a trend is apparent (high ADX value). But, only a certain time of the day for signals is allowed. For example, if you are trading energies, maybe the appropriate breakout times are 10:30 – 11:30 AM Eastern time. For stocks, maybe the correct time is after the opening, say 9:45 – 10:45 AM Eastern.

Obviously, restricting the breakout signal to more "meaningful" times adds a level of complexity, but also can create a better entry signal. You just have to test it and see!

Tradestation Code

```
Var: tbeg(945); // signal window start time
Var: tend(1045); //signal window end time
Var: offset(.1); //additional amount the price has to break the high or
low before entering a trade – can be zero if desired
Var: adxP(10); // ADX lookback period
Var: adxThresh(20); // ADX threshold for signifying a trend

if time>=tbeg and time<=tend then begin
if EntriesToday(date[o])<1 and adx (adxP) >= AdxThresh  then begin
buy next bar at highd(1) + Offset Points stop;
sellshort next bar at lowd(1) - Offset points stop;
end;
end;
```

Plain English Code

First, make sure the current bar time is between *tbeg* and *tend*. That window is the only time valid trade signals are allowed.

Next, make sure there have been no other entries today (this of course can be changed to limit it to any number of maximum desired entries).

Lastly, calculate the ADX indicator for the last *adxP* bars. If that value is above *AdxThresh*, there is a significant trend present, and trades can be taken.

Assuming all of the above are acceptable, long and short trade orders can be placed. The buy trade order will be a stop order at the previous day's high plus the *offset* value. For a sell short order, it will be at the previous day's low minus the *offset*. Both orders are using stops.

Entry #7 with a simple profit target and stop loss

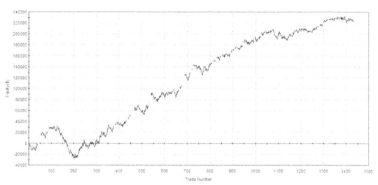

Equity Curve Line - @RB 15 min.(01/01/07 22:46 - 04/17/19 15:30)

ENTRY #8 – "INTRADAY BREAKOUT WITH EXPANDING RANGE"

General Concept

This entry is exactly the same as Entry #7, with one additional condition. The range of yesterday must be greater than the range of two days ago. The idea here is that the range expansion in last few days is likely to continue, in the same way that up days beget more up days.

This entry is designed for very short term intraday breakouts. This will not work on daily charts, since there are specific bar times when this pattern can be active.

It is just a simple breakout of highs and lows – you will enter in the direction of the breakout. There is also an ADX filter, so you will be entering only if a trend is apparent (high ADX value). But, only a certain time of the day for signals is allowed. For example, if you are trading energies, maybe the appropriate breakout times are 10:30 – 11:30 AM Eastern time. For stocks, maybe the correct time is after the opening, say 9:45 – 10:45 AM Eastern.

Obviously, restricting the breakout signal to more "meaningful" times adds a level of complexity, but also can create a better entry signal. You just have to test it and see!

Tradestation Code

Var: tbeg(945); // signal window start time

Var: tend(1045); //signal window end time

Var: offset(.1); //additional amount the price has to break the high or low before entering a trade – can be zero if desired

Var: adxP(10); // ADX lookback period

Var: adxThresh(20); // ADX threshold for signifying a trend

if time>=tbeg and time<=tend then begin

if EntriesToday(date[o])<1 and adx (adxP) >= AdxThresh and (highd(1)-lowd(1) > highd(2)-lowd(2)) then begin

buy next bar at highd(1) + Offset Points stop;

sellshort next bar at lowd(1) - Offset points stop;

end;

end;

Plain English Code

First, make sure the current bar time is between *tbeg* and *tend*. That window is the only time valid trade signals are allowed.

Next, make sure there have been no other entries today (this of course can be changed to limit it to any number of maximum desired entries).

Also, the range of yesterday [high yesterday minus low yesterday] must be larger than the range 2 days ago [high 2 days ago minus the low 2 days ago].

Lastly, calculate the ADX indicator for the last *adxP* bars. If that value is above *AdxThresh*, there is a significant trend present, and trades can be taken.

Assuming all of the above are acceptable, long and short trade orders can be placed. The buy trade order will be a stop order at the previous day's high plus the *offset* value. For a sell short order, it will be at the previous day's low minus the *offset*. Both orders are using stops.

ENTRY #9 – "DAY OF WEEK TRADING"

General Concept

If you have traded long enough, you may have noticed certain markets tend to perform better or worse on certain days, as compared to other days. Maybe it is because of regularly scheduled government reports, or maybe for other reasons, but this does seem to be true.

This code takes advantage of any daily biases that are present.

One word of caution though – don't try to use this code to optimize the day of the week. You might find through optimization, for example, that Gold performs better on Tuesday than any other day. That could be significant, but it also could be because in a test of Monday – Friday, one day will always be better than the others. Is it real, or just an artifact of the optimization test?

So, when I use this sort of code, I always like to have a reason why that particular day does better. Ideally, I have the reason BEFORE I run the test.

Here is an example: the weekly energy report comes out on Wednesdays: https://www.eia.gov/petroleum/supply/weekly/

So you may decide that any significant price movements on Wednesdays (and only Wednesday) are what this strategy should trade. That is sound logic.

An approach like that is much better than just optimizing for day of the week.

A good source of reports can be found here: https://www.investing.com/economic-calendar/

This particular entry uses time of day as an additional trigger, so you need to use minute bars with it. You could also use daily bars, if you remove the time constraint.

Tradestation Code

If time=935 and dayofweek(date)= 3 then Buy next bar at highd(1) stop;

If time=935 and dayofweek(date)= 4 then SellShort next bar at lowd(1) stop;

Plain English Code

At 9:35 on Wednesdays, buy the next bar on a stop at yesterday's high. On Thursdays, sell short at yesterday's low.

Note that as written, this code will not generate many trades. Not only is the order valid for only one bar (the bar after the 935 bar), but the price has to be above or below yesterday's high or low during the 935 bar. So, do not be surprised if the trades are infrequent.

ENTRY #10 – "ENHANCED DAY OF WEEK TRADING"

General Concept

Make sure you review and understand Entry #9 before employing this entry. It is just Entry #9, with an additional condition added to it.

The reason I am showing this (besides the fact that testing has shown it works) is that this is the way you should think of all entries – adding and subtracting conditions , filters, constraints, etc. In your own development, you should definitely modify these entries to add your favorite ideas (I used momentum in this modification, since I have found momentum to be very useful).

Tradestation Code

```
Var: xbars(10); // lookback period for momentum
```

If time=935 and dayofweek(date)= 3 and close>close[xbars] then Buy next bar at highd(1) stop;

If time=935 and dayofweek(date)= 4 and close<close[xbars] then SellShort next bar at lowd(1) stop;

Plain English Code

At 9:35 on Wednesdays, and if the current close is greater than the close *xbars* ago, buy the next bar on a stop at yesterday's high. On Thursdays, sell short at yesterday's low, only if the current close is less than the close *xbars* ago.

This will produce even fewer trades than Entry #9, so be careful!

ENTRY #11 – "NOT DAY OF WEEK TRADING"

General Concept

In Entry #9, we chose a specific day to take trades. What if the opposite is true? Maybe instead of entering a long trade on Thursday, maybe every day except Thursday is good to enter longs.

This code excludes a certain day of the week. In this case, we can take long trades every day except Wednesday, and we can take short trades every day except Thursday.

Again, just like I recommended for Entry #9, you ideally want a valid reason for including or excluding certain days of the week. Without the valid reason, any optimization "best" day you discover might just be the result of data mining bias.

Tradestation Code

If dayofweek(date)<> 3 then Buy next bar at highd(1) stop;
If dayofweek(date)<> 4 then SellShort next bar at lowd(1) stop;

Plain English Code

On every day except Wednesday, buy the next bar on a stop at yesterday's high. On every day except Thursdays, sell short at yesterday's low.

ENTRY #12 – "RSI TRIGGER"

General Concept

RSI is a classic indicator, the Relative Strength Index, developed by Welles Wilder. I have found it useful to use in many strategies.

The RSI traditionally signals overbought and oversold regions. Any value above 70-80 signals an overbought condition, where a correction downwards might be forthcoming. Any value below 20-30 suggests an oversold condition, where the price could be poised for a rebound.

I don't want to debate whether or not indicators like RSI actually work or not. In some cases they do, but in other cases they do not. As I have mentioned many times, this is something you have to test. Once you see the profit or loss from your backtest, you will know whether or not the RSI works in that specific situation.

I have used this entry with stocks, ETFs and stock indices.

Tradestation Code

Var: RSILength(5); //RSI lookback period
Var: RSIThreshold(80); //RSI threshold
Var: XBars(5); //moving average lookback period

If   RSI(Close,RSILength)<   RSIThreshold   And   Close   >
Average(Close,Xbars) Then buy next bar at market;
　　If   RSI(Close,RSILength)>   100-RSIThreshold   And   Close   <
Average(Close,Xbars) Then Sellshort next bar at market;

Plain English Code

First, calculate the RSI over the last *RSILength* bars.

If the RSI is below *RSIThreshold*, and the close is greater than the average close over the last *Xbars*, then buy at the next market open.

If the RSI is above 100 minus the *RSIThreshold*, and the close is less than the average close over the last *Xbars*, then sell short at the next market open.

ENTRY #13 – "MOVING AVERAGE CROSS, WITH A TWIST"

General Concept

Practically everyone knows the standard moving average crossover signal. If the fast moving average crosses above the slower (longer period) moving average, it is time to buy. Vice versa for short trades.

This type of signal used to work pretty well, but as new algo traders entered the scene, practically everyone and their mother and grandmother and even great grandmother started trading it! This reduced the usefulness of the signal.

But all is not lost. This entry has worked well, even though it is based on this "old" signal. It just adds a twist to it – it will only take the moving average cross if the current close has not run away from the previous bar's low. This eliminates some of the crosses due to price spikes, which might just be a temporary overshoot or undershoot.

I have used this entry with softs and agricultural futures.

Tradestation Code

Var: FastLength (10), SlowLength(20); // moving average lengths
Var: XX(3); // threshold (measured in price of instrument) for valid signals

If Average(Close, FastLength) crosses above Average(Close, SlowLength) and close<low[1]+ XX then Buy next bar at market;
If Average(Close, FastLength) crosses below Average(Close, SlowLength) and close>high[1] - XX then Sell Short next bar at market;

Plain English Code

First, calculate the fast and slow moving averages.

Next, if the fast length moving average crosses above the slow length moving average, and the current close is below the low plus the threshold, then buy the next bar at market.

If the fast length moving average crosses below the slow length moving average, and the current close is above the high minus the threshold, then sell short the next bar at market.

ENTRY #14 – "SPLIT WEEK, PART 1"

General Concept

In an earlier entry, I discussed trading based on a certain day of the week. This entry takes that idea, and expands on it. The concept is that mid–week trading (Tuesday, Wednesday, Thursday) is different than days before or after a weekend (Friday, Monday).

Entry 14 can generate signals on Tuesday, Wednesday or Thursday.

This entry looks for the highest high and the highest close before a buy is initiated, with the reverse for a sell short signal. An added condition is a volatility filter, designed to ignore signals during high volatility (as measured by the average true range) situations.

I have used this entry with metals and currencies.

Tradestation Code

Var: bbars(15); // lookbar period for the recent highest and lowest prices

Var: maxl(2500); // max allowable average true range, converted to dollars per contract

Condition1 = dayofweek(date)=2 or dayofweek(date)=3 or dayofweek(date)=4; //True or False

If Condition1 and high=highest(high,bbars) and close=highest(close,bbars) and avgtruerange(14)*BigPointValue<maxl then buy next bar at market;

If Condition1 and low=lowest(low,bbars) and close=lowest(close,bbars) and avgtruerange(14)*BigPointValue<maxl then sellshort next bar at market;

Plain English Code

Start out by determining what day of the week the current bar is. Ignore any day except Tuesday, Wednesday and Thursday.

Assuming the day of the week is matched, if the high of the current bar is the highest high of the last *bbars*, and the close is the highest close of the *bbars*, a long signal is initiated only if the 14 period average true range multiplied by the dollar value per point is below *maxl*.

Multiplying the average true range by the dollar value per point converts it to a dollar amount per contract. This allows us to take only low volatility trades, regardless of market.

Entry #14 with a trailing exit

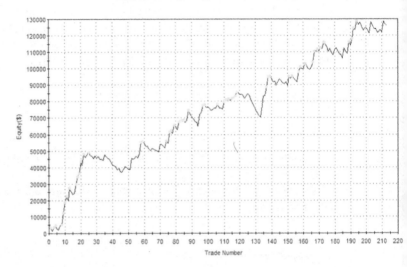

Equity Curve Line - @PL Daily(01/02/07 17:00 - 04/11/19 17:00)

ENTRY #15 – "SPLIT WEEK, PART 2"

General Concept

While the previous entry was for mid-week, this entry is specifically for Friday and Monday, where the weekend effects showing up on Friday or Monday will be taken into account.

Entry 15 can generate signals on Friday or Monday.

This entry looks for the highest high and the highest close before a buy is initiated, with the reverse for a sell short signal. An added condition is a volatility filter, designed to ignore signals during high volatility (as measure by the average true range) situations.

I have used this entry with metals and currencies.

Tradestation Code

Var: bbars(15); // lookbar period for the recent highest and lowest prices

Var: maxl(2500); // max allowable average true range, converted to dollars per contract

Condition1 = dayofweek(date)=5 or dayofweek(date)=1; //True or False

If Condition1 and high=highest(high,bbars) and close=highest(close,bbars) and avgtruerange(14)*BigPointValue<maxl then buy next bar at market;

If Condition1 and low=lowest(low,bbars) and close=lowest(close,bbars) and avgtruerange(14)*BigPointValue<maxl then sellshort next bar at market;

Plain English Code

Start out by determining what day of the week the current bar is. Ignore any day except Friday or Monday.

Assuming the day of the week is matched, if the high of the current bar is the highest high of the last *bbars*, and the close is the highest close of the *bbars*, a long signal is initiated only if the 14 period average true range multiplied by the dollar value per point is below *maxl*.

Multiplying the average true range by the dollar value per point converts it to a dollar amount per contract. This allows us to take only low volatility trades, regardless of market.

ENTRY #16 – "INTRODUCING SERIAL CORRELATION"

General Concept

For most trading strategies, one trade does not depend on any other previous trade. The trades are completely independent. This is true of most strategies developed using patterns, or indicators, or even statistics.

But, let's say you want to only enter a trade after a number of days if the last trade was profitable? And maybe, you wait a longer or shorter period if the last trade was not profitable.

Such an idea might be good for long term trend following approaches. For example, it is not very common for a profitable long signal to be followed by another profitable long signal or a profitable short signal. Many times, the signal immediately after a big win will not work as the market consolidates and takes a breather. So it is better to wait.

Also, sometimes the strategy just gets out of sync with the market. To combat this, the entry waits even longer to enter the next trade.

Note that the waiting period lengths for the next trade can be variables, and can be reversed – where you wait longer after a profitable trade, for example. I recommend testing to see what works best for your situation.

This strategy takes advantage of this phenomenon, with a simple countertrend approach (buying the lowest recent close, selling short for the highest recent close).

Tradestation Code

Var: xbars(15); // lookback period

If ((PositionProfit(1)>0 and BarsSinceExit(1)>=5) //if last position was profitable, wait 5 bars before taking a new trade
or (PositionProfit(1)<=0 and BarsSinceExit(1)>=20) // if last trade was a loser, wait 20 bars before taking the next signal

or TotalTrades=0) then begin //allows the first trade in the backtest
to occur

if Close = Lowest(Close, xbars) then buy next bar at market;
if Close = Highest(Close, xbars) then SellShort next bar at market;
end;

Plain English Code

If you have not taken any trades, then all signals are valid. If the last trade was profitable and it exited more than 5 bars ago, you are cleared to take the next trade. Also, if the last trade was a loser, and 20 bars have elapsed since that position's exit, you can also take the next signal.

Assuming one of the previous three conditions is true, then go long if the current close is equal to the lowest close of the last *xbars*. Do the exact opposite for short entries.

ENTRY #17 – "BACK IN STYLE"

General Concept

The entry is based off of a pattern. In this case I know that I was not the original creator!

That is pretty typical of a lot of entries that I use. I find something – in a book, a trading magazine, the Internet – and then play around with it, modify it to suit my needs, test it, etc. Sometimes the original idea becomes highly modified, and sometimes it stays exactly the same.

This entry has 2 significant modifications from Michael Harris, and his great book "Profitability and Systematic Trading: A Quantitative Approach to Profitability, Risk, and Money Management." This book was written over 10 years ago, so any idea you test right off the bat can have 10 years of true out of sample testing!

I call this entry "back in style" because it worked well with stocks in the early 2000s, and faltered from 2011 to 2017. In 2018, it made a roaring comeback though. Of course, the performance could also be due to the exits I used.

Tradestation Code

if (l[3] > h[0] AND h[0] > l[1] AND l[0] > l[2] AND l[1] > l[2]) then sellshort Next Bar at open;

if (h[3] < l[0] AND l[0] < h[1] AND h[0] < h[2] AND h[1] < h[2]) then buy Next Bar at open;

Plain English Code

If the low 3 bars ago is greater than the current high, and the current high is greater than the previous bar low, and the current bar low is greater than the low 2 bars ago and the previous bar low is greater than the low 2 bars ago, sell short at the next market open.

Do the exact opposite for long entries, using highs instead of lows.

ENTRY #18 – "WHERE YOU AT?"

General Concept

This entry is based on where the current close is relative to the very recent highs and lows. In that respect, it is basically a stochastic calculation. https://www.investopedia.com/terms/s/stochasticoscillator.asp

If the close is in the upper part of the range, it goes short. If it is in the lower range, it goes long.

It works well in stocks and stock indices, because it basically is a mean reverting type entry (buy weakness, sell strength).

As an added feature, it disregards any signals in the early nighttime hours (applicable to 24 hour futures markets only).

Tradestation Code

```
Var: ll(0), hh(0);
Var: Thresh(.5); // threshold value for entries, between 0 and 1

if time<1600 or time>2300 then begin

ll=minlist(l,l[1]);
hh=maxlist(h,h[1]);

if (c-ll)/(hh-ll+.000001)>=thresh then sellshort next bar at market;
if (c-ll)/(hh-ll+.000001)<=(1-thresh) then buy next bar at market;
end;
```

Plain English Code

First ensure that the current bar time is not between 1600 and 2300, exchange time.

Next calculate the variable ll, which is the lowest low of the current low and previous bar low. Also, calculate the variable hh, which is the highest high of the current bar and the previous bar.

Finally calculate the position of the current close. Take the current close minus variable ll, and divide it by the difference $hh-ll$. The result should be between 0 and 1 always (if it is not, check your calculations or data).

If the calculated value is greater than the $thresh$ variable, sell short at the next bar. If the value is less than 1 minus the $thresh$ variable, buy the next bar at market.

Entry #18 with a simple profit target

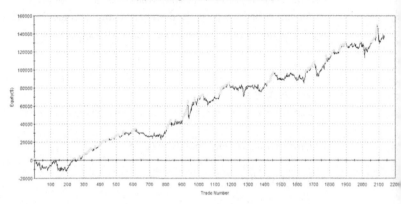

Equity Curve Line - @ES 60 min.(06/03/01 18:00 - 04/12/19 08:30)

ENTRY #19 –
"EXPONENTIALLY BETTER"

General Concept

Up until this point, I have only discussed simple moving averages. I like those because of their simplicity. Of course, there are dozens of other types of moving averages, each of which claims to remedy some flaw in the simple moving average.

The truth is there is no perfect moving average type – each one has its flaws and its perks.

This strategy uses a dual exponential moving average crossover to generate signals.

This could be used on any market, but I originally used it with metals.

Tradestation Code

```
var:avg1(10),avg2(20); // 2 exponential moving averages
var:lookbackdays(10); // lengths of faster exponential moving average


avg1=xaverage(close,lookbackdays);
avg2=xaverage(close,lookbackdays*4); //slower average has length 4 x the faster average

Condition1 = (avg1>avg2 and avg1[1]<avg2[1]);
If Condition1 then Buy next bar at high stop;

Condition2 = (avg1<avg2 and avg1[1]>avg2[1]);
If Condition2 then SellShort next bar at low stop;
```

Plain English Code

Using a length of *lookbackdays*, calculate a faster exponential moving average, and with a length of 4 * *lookbackdays*, calculate a slower exponential moving average.

When the fast average crosses above the slow average, buy the next bar on a stop at the current bar high.

When the fast average crosses below the slow average, sell short the next bar on a stop at the current bar low.

ENTRY #20 – "RANGE BREAKOUT"

General Concept

Breakout comes in many types and styles. You can have a breakout based just on a price, or a price plus or minus some calculated value. Sometimes I like using the daily range as an entry, with non-daily bars.

This entry first identifies a new trading day (measured by calendar day, not session) and then grabs the open price, along with calculating the range of the previous day.

Once these initial calculations are done (on the first bar of the next day), the breakout points are set. As an additional feature, the strategy only allows entry before 1300 time.

Tradestation Code

```
var:xfl(.1),xfs(.1);
var:rangeavg(0),yesterdayclose01(0),yesterdayclose02(0),todayopen
(0),daylow(0),dayhigh(0),range10(0),range09(0),range08(0),range07(
0),range06(0),range05(0),range04(0),range03(0),range02(0),range01(
0);
If date<>date[1] then begin //close of first bar of day
//new day, reset high and low, and shift all ranges

todayopen=open;
yesterdayclose02=yesterdayclose01; //close 2 days ago
yesterdayclose01=close[1]; //close yesterday

range10=range09;
range09=range08;
range08=range07;
range07=range06;
range06=range05;
range05=range04;
range04=range03;
range03=range02;
range02=range01;

//range01 is the true range of yesterday, calculated at the close of the
first bar today
range01=maxlist(absvalue(dayhigh-
yesterdayclose02),absvalue(daylow-yesterdayclose02),dayhigh-
daylow);

daylow=99999.;
```

dayhigh=-99999.;

end;

rangeavg=(range10+range09+range08+range07+range06+range05 +range04+range03+range02+range01)/10.;

If high>Dayhigh then dayhigh=high;
If low<daylow then daylow=low;

//entry signals

If Time <1300 then begin
Buy next bar at todayopen + xfl*rangeavg stop;
SellShort next bar at todayopen - xfs*rangeavg stop;
End;

Plain English Code

At the first bar of a new calendar, first calculate the range (not the average true range) of the previous day (not just the previous bar). Then, calculate the average range over the last 10 days.

For time of day between midnight and 1300, buy the next bar at today's open plus *xfl* times the average range. Also, sell short the next bar at today's open minus *xfs* times the average range.

ENTRY #21 – "ASYMMETRIC TRIPLE"

General Concept

Occasionally I create entries that work well, but I do not particularly like. Such is the case with this entry. It has two things I do not like. First, it has an asymmetric entry for long and short. I usually like the long and short to be exactly opposite. Second, it uses a triple average, which is really an average of an average. A little bit different, to say the least!

I used this entry on a foreign stock market index.

Tradestation Code

```
var: EntryL(0),EntryS(0),ATRmult(0), Length1(10),Length2(12);
var: EntCondL(False), EntCondS(False);

EntryL = C + ATRmult * AvgTrueRange(14);
EntryS = LowD(0) - ATRmult * AvgTrueRange(14);

Value1 = TriAverage(LowD(0), Length1);
Value2= L[Length2];
EntCondL = Value1>=Value2;
EntCondS = true;

If EntCondL then  Buy next bar at EntryL stop;
If EntCondS then  SellShort next bar at EntryS stop;
```

Plain English Code

First calculate the long and short entry prices. The long entry price is the current bar close plus *ATRmult* times the 14 period Average True Range. The short entry price is the day's low minus *ATRmult* times the 14 period Average True Range. Note that these are not symmetric prices.

Then, calculate the triple average of daily lows for the lookback period of *Length1*. If that value is greater than the low of *Length2* bars ago, then you can place a long order. Otherwise, no long order can be placed.

The short order can always be placed.

Finally, if a long entry is possible, buy the next bar at *EntryL* on a stop. Similarly, sell short the next bar at *EntryS* on a stop.

ENTRY #22 – "ASYMMETRIC AGAIN"

General Concept

Here is another asymmetric entry. Obviously, you could come up with all sorts of variations on this – both symmetric and asymmetric. As I mentioned, I am not a huge fan of these.

Why?

Having separate calculation methods for long and short entries leads to more degrees of freedom in the strategy. Simply put, there are more things possible to tweak and optimize. More optimization will yield better backtest results, but my experience is that does not usually work well going forward in real time.

So, if you must use asymmetric entries, make sure first the market is amenable to it (like the stock market, which has an upward bias), then use it with minimal optimization.

Tradestation Code

```
var: EntryL(0),EntryS(0),ATRmult(0);
var: EntCondL(False), EntCondS(False);

EntryL = OpenD(0) + ATRmult * AvgTrueRange(14);
EntryS = LowD(0) - ATRmult * AvgTrueRange(14);

Value1 = OpenD(0);
Value2= CloseD(1);
EntCondL = Value1>=Value2;
EntCondS = true;

If EntCondL then  Buy next bar at EntryL stop;
If EntCondS then  SellShort next bar at EntryS stop;
```

Plain English Code

First calculate the long and short entry prices. The long entry price is the daily open plus *ATRmult* times the 14 period Average True Range. The short entry price is the day's low minus *ATRmult* times the 14 period Average True Range. Note that these are not symmetric prices.

If today's open is greater than yesterday's close then you can place a long order. Otherwise, no long order can be placed.

The short order can always be placed.

Finally, if a long entry is possible, buy the next bar at *EntryL* on a stop. Similarly, sell short the next bar at *EntryS* on a stop.

ENTRY #23 – "STOCHASTIC CROSS"

General Concept

The Stochastic Indicator is a fairly popular one, and many people use it as a confirmation filter of a primary signal. But it can also be used on its own as a signal generator.

In this entry, I simply look for a cross of the stochastic %k and %d lines. If you are unfamiliar with what those are, I recommend consulting this article: https://www.investopedia.com/terms/s/stochasticoscillator.asp

Tradestation Code

Vars: SLength(8), Smoothing1(23), Smoothing2(22);
Vars: Smoothingtype(1), oFastK(0), oFastD(0), oSlowK(0), oSlowD(0) ;

Value1 = Stochastic(H, L, C, SLength, Smoothing1,
Smoothing2, SmoothingType, oFastK, oFastD, oSlowK, oSlowD) ;

if oSlowk crosses over oSlowd then buy next bar at market;
if oSlowk crosses under oSlowd then sellshort next bar at market;

Plain English Code

Calculate the %k and %d stochastics, using inputs *Slength*, *Smoothing1* and *Smoothing2*. Most trading software has a built in stochastic function to assist with this.

Then, if the %k crosses over the %d value, buy the next bar at market. If the %k crosses under the %d value, sell short the next bar at market.

Entry #23, With Simple Stop Loss

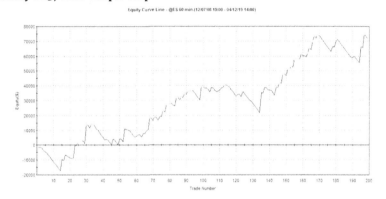

Equity Curve Line - @ES 60 min.(12/07/98 19:00 - 04/12/19 14:00)

ENTRY #24 – "SHOW ME THE MONEY (FLOW)"

General Concept

The MoneyFlow indicator, standard in many software packages (described   here: https://en.wikipedia.org/wiki/Money_flow_index), is a calculation that varies from 0 to 100, and is a proxy to represent the money coming in or out of the market.

Much like RSI, the MoneyFlow indicator has overbought and oversold regions, and buys and sells accordingly.

Tradestation Code

Vars: Length(14),OverSold(20),Overbought(80);
vars: MoneyFlowVal(0) ;

MoneyFlowVal = MoneyFlow(Length) ;

if MoneyFlowVal Crosses above OverSold then buy next bar at market;
if MoneyFlowVal Crosses below Overbought then Sellshort next bar at market;

Plain English Code

Calculate the MoneyFlow Indicator using a length of 14.

Then, if the *MoneyFlowVal* crosses above 20, buy the next bar at market. If the *MoneyFlowVal* crosses under 80, sell short the next bar at market.

ENTRY #25 – "CLASSIC BOLLINGER BANDS"

General Concept

As the title suggests, this entry uses the Bollinger Band indicator to signal an entry. I add two things that I have found useful. First, I add a simple momentum condition. Second, I simply enter with a market order.

Tradestation Code

vars: Length(20), NumDevs(2), Length2(10);
vars: LowerBand(0), UpperBand(0);

LowerBand = BollingerBand(Close, Length, -NumDevs) ;
UpperBand = BollingerBand(Close, Length, +NumDevs) ;

if Close crosses over LowerBand and close>close[Length2] then Buy next bar at market;
if Close crosses under UpperBand and close<close[Length2] then SellShort next bar at market;

Plain English Code

Calculate the upper and lower Bollinger Bands over the past Length bars, using a standard deviation of plus or minus *NumDevs*. If the close of the current bar crosses over the lower band, then buy the next bar. If the close of the current bar crosses under the upper band, then sell short the next bar. Also, the *Length2* length momentum must be going in the same direction as the signal -- *close>close[Length2]* for buy signal, vice versa for short.

ENTRY #26 – "CLASSIC KELTNER CHANNEL"

General Concept

As the title suggests, this entry uses the Keltner Channel indicator to signal an entry. As with the Bollinger Band, which is pretty similar, I add two things that I have found useful. First, I add a simple momentum condition. Second, I simply enter with a market order.

Tradestation Code

vars: Length(20), NumATRs(2), Length2(10);
vars: LowerBand(0), UpperBand(0);

LowerBand = Average(close,Length)-NumATRs*AvgTrueRange(Length) ;
UpperBand = Average(close,Length)+NumATRs*AvgTrueRange(Length) ;

if Close crosses over LowerBand and close>close[Length2] then Buy next bar at market;
if Close crosses under UpperBand and close<close[Length2] then SellShort next bar at market;

Plain English Code

Calculate the upper and lower Keltner Channels over the past Length bars, using an average true range of plus or minus *NumATRs*. If the close of the current bar crosses over the lower band, then buy the next bar. If the close of the current bar crosses under the upper band, then sell short the next bar. Also, the *Length2* length momentum must be going in the same direction as the signal -- *close>close[Length2]* for buy signal, vice versa for short.

DANGER – WARNING!

Since this is the halfway point of the book, I wanted to point out a few things before I reveal the rest of the entries and exits.

Be careful with the entries and exits in this book!

What do I mean by that?

Simply put, these entries and exits are not exactly "plug and play" ready. They are very useful pieces in your strategy building process, and will likely save you hundreds or thousands of hours in time, but they are not a finished product.

You can't just simply grab an entry, and grab an exit, throw them on a chart and start trading. That would be foolish.

And you can't just take the entries and exits, optimize them over all your historic data, take the best parameter set, and start trading. That would be even more foolish. DON'T OVER-OPTIMIZE!

I know both of those approaches are terrible, because I did them both earlier in my trading journey. As you might well imagine, both ended badly.

Don't be the me of 20 years ago!

If you are serious about trading, be like the current day me:

1. I have a set process to test and evaluate every potential trading strategy, BEFORE I allocate real capital to it.

2. The process I use has proven itself over time, and many traders have also been successful with it. It is the process I used to win the trading championships.

3. I realize that even with a solid process, most trading strategies will not work – they will not pass my tests. That is frustrating, but it is OK.

4. The strategy development process is never ending. Even today, after all these years, I still test new strategies all the time. Markets evolve, and a good trader tries to keep up.

5. The entries and exits in this book are a great starting point, but how you work with them to create a viable strategy is really the key.

I hope that helps you a bit, especially if you are eager to trade. Patience is important in developing a strategy!

Now, back to the entries and exits...

ENTRY #27 – "THREE AMIGOS"

General Concept

Sometimes bringing multiple entry techniques together yields some good results. I have used this with currencies and metals. It uses the RSI indicator, the ADX indicator and short and long term momentum calculations.

Be careful when using these types of "composite" entries, since the urge to optimize all parameters is huge. When you use them, try to optimize as little as possible.

Tradestation Code

```
vars:      ADXLength(14),      RSILength(14),      lookbackBig(20),
lookbackshort(10);

If ADX(ADXLength)>25 then begin
    If  RSI(close,RSILength)<50  and  close<close[lookbackBig]  and
close>close[lookbackshort] then buy next bar at market;
    If  RSI(close,RSILength)>50  and  close>close[lookbackBig]  and
close<close[lookbackshort] then sellshort next bar at market;
    end;
```

Plain English Code

Calculate the ADX with length *ADXlength*. If it is less than 25 (non-trending condition), do not take any trades.

If the ADX is greater than 25:

If RSI of length *RSILength* is below 50, and the close is less than the close *lookbackBig* bars ago, and the close is greater than the close of *lookbackshort* bars ago, then buy the next bar at market;

If RSI of length *RSILength* is above 50, and the close is greater than the close *lookbackBig* bars ago, and the close is less than the close of *lookbackshort* bars ago, then sell short the next bar at market;

ENTRY #28 – "TWO AMIGOS"

General Concept

This entry uses ADX, which has been used with many other entries, along with a simple momentum. Of course, you could try of variations with this. Besides trying different parameter values, you could change the ">" symbols with "<" to make it a countertrend strategy, for example.

Tradestation Code

```
vars: ADXLength(14), lookback(20);

If ADX(ADXLength)>20 then begin
If close>close[lookback] then buy next bar at market;
If close<close[lookback] then sellshort next bar at market;
end;
```

Plain English Code

Calculate the ADX with length ADXlength. If it is less than 20 (non-trending condition), do not take any trades.

If the ADX is greater than 20:

If the close is greater than the close *lookback* bars ago, then buy the next bar at market;

If the close is less than the close *lookback* bars ago, then sell short the next bar at market;

ENTRY #29 – "PITTER PATTER PATTERN"

General Concept

I like simple patterns, and this one is no exception. I use this on daily Unleaded Gas, but you should try it on a variety of other markets and bar sizes. You never know where it is going to work until you test and evaluate it. This was based on Michael Harris' work once again. I removed roughly half of his conditions, and I also made it bi-directional.

Tradestation Code

If o[1] > h[o] AND o[o] > c[1] AND c[1] > l[1] AND l[1] > c[o] then buy next bar at market;

if o[1] < l[o] AND o[o] < c[1] AND c[1] < h[1] AND h[1] < c[o] then sell short next bar at market;

Plain English Code

Long trades: previous open >current high AND current open > previous close AND previous close > previous low AND previous low > current close

Short trades: change all "high" with "low" and all ">" with "<"

ENTRY #30 – "PITTER PATTER PATTERN 2"

General Concept

Another, slightly simpler, pattern – similar to Entry 17, but with signals reversed and another condition added. What is nice about simple patterns like this is that you are less likely to optimize them, as compared to say a moving average length. You could optimize the number of bars back, but I do not recommend it.

Tradestation Code

If $l[3]>h[o]$ and $h[o]>l[1]$ and $l[1]>l[2]$ and $c[o] > c[1]$ then buy next bar at market;

If $h[3]<l[o]$ and $l[o]<h[1]$ and $h[1]<h[2]$ and $c[o] < c[1]$ then sell short next bar at market;

Plain English Code

Long trades: low 3 bars ago > current high AND current high > previous low AND previous low > low 2 bars ago AND current close > previous close

Short trades: change all "high" with "low" and all ">" with "<"

ENTRY #31 – "CLOSING PATTERN ONLY"

General Concept

Here is another pattern, just based on the pattern of recent closes. It is not as simple as 5 consecutive up closes or anything like that, but it is fairly easy to understand.

I have used this in the metals sector.

The exact opposite pattern can also work, too. I have used the opposite in the energy sector.

Tradestation Code

if c[1]>c[3] and c>c[2] and c[2]>c[1] then buy next bar at market;

If c[1]<c[3] and c<c[2] and c[2]<c[1] then Sell short next bar at market;

Plain English Code

Long trades: close 1 bar ago is greater than close 3 bars ago AND current close is greater than close 2 bars ago AND close 2 bars ago is greater than close 1 bar ago. Short trades: change all all ">" with "<"

ENTRY #32 – "QUICK PULLBACK PATTERN"

General Concept

The idea behind this small pattern is that you have a high 2 bars ago, followed by a lower high, which can be thought of as a consolidation or a pullback, followed by a close above that initial high. The higher low helps confirms the signal. Put everything together, and it is a good time to buy.

I have used this with energies with some success.

Tradestation Code

if h[2]>h[1] and l[2]<l[1] and c>h[2] then buy next bar at market;

if l[2]<l[1] and h[2]>h[1] and c<l[2] then sell   short next bar at market;

Plain English Code

To generate a long trade signal, the following pieces have to be in place:

High 2 bars ago greater than the high 1 bar ago

AND

Low 2 bars ago less than the low 1 bar ago

AND

The current close greater than the high 2 bars ago.

For a short signal, it is just the reverse:

Low 2 bars ago less than the low 1 bar ago

AND

High 2 bars ago greater than the high 1 bar ago

AND

The current close less than the low 2 bars ago.

Entry #32 with simple profit target, stop loss and time exit

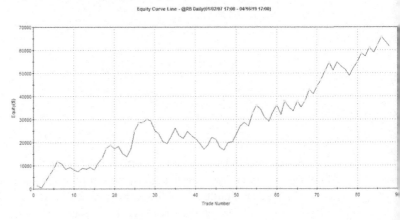

Equity Curve Line - @RB Daily(01/02/07 17:00 - 04/16/19 17:00)

ENTRY #33 – "CLOSING PATTERN ONLY II"

General Concept

Here is another closing price pattern, just based on the pattern of recent closes. It is not as simple as 5 consecutive up closes or anything like that, but it is fairly easy to understand.

I have used this in the interest rate sector, with non-daily bars.

Tradestation Code

if $c[1]<c[2]$ and $c[2]<c[5]$ and $c[5]<c[3]$ and $c[3]<c[4]$ then buy next bar at market;

If $c[1]>c[2]$ and $c[2]>c[5]$ and $c[5]>c[3]$ and $c[3]>c[4]$ then Sell short next bar at market;

Plain English Code

Long trades: close 2 bars ago is greater than close 1 bar ago and close 2 bars ago is less than close 5 bars ago AND close 5 bars ago is less than close 3 bars ago and close 3 bars ago is less than close 4 bars ago.

Short trades: change all all ">" with "<"

Entry #33 with simple profit target, stop loss and time exit

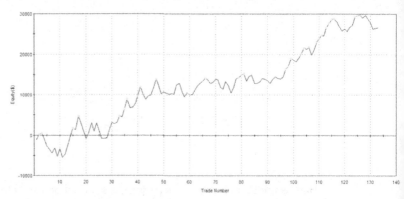

ENTRY #34 – "BREAKDOWN DEAD AHEAD"

General Concept

This entry looks pretty simple, but it is a pretty neat idea. It looks for a breakdown in the current trend, as measured by simple momentum. If the price moves far enough away from the previous close, it suggests a change in trend, or possibly a countertrend move.

I have used this in a few Softs markets.

Tradestation Code

Var: momen(10); //length of trend
Var: mult(2); //multiplier for the average true range
var:myrange(0);

myrange=truerange; //true range is a Tradestation reserved word

If close>close[momen] then sellshort next bar at close-mult*average(myRange,3) stop;

If close<close[momen] then buy next bar at close+mult*average(myRange,3) stop;

Plain English Code

First calculate the current bar's true range, and put it in variable *myrange.*

Then, if the *momen* length momentum is positive, place an order to sell short the next bar at the current close minus the term (*mult* * 3 period average of true range) on a stop.

Finally, if the *momen* length momentum is negative, place an order to buy the next bar at the current close plus the term (*mult* * 3 period average of true range) on a stop.

ENTRY #35 – "COMMODITY CHANNEL INDEX"

General Concept

The Commodity Channel Index is a semi-popular indicator, created back in 1980.
https://en.wikipedia.org/wiki/Commodity_channel_index

Although many times people use this with other calculations, for this simple strategy I just use it by itself, with no other calculation or indicator. Of course, you could always others in, but I have found that in some situations this works pretty well by itself.

I have used this in the currency markets.

Tradestation Code

input: CCILength(14),CCIAvgLength(9);
vars: CCIValue(0),CCIAvg(0);

CCIValue = CCI(CCILength) ;
CCIAvg = Average(CCIValue, CCIAvgLength);

if CCIAvg>=100 then sell short next bar at open;
if CCIAvg<=-100 then buy next bar at open;

Plain English Code

Start out by calculating the CCI for the period *CCILength*.

Next, calculate the *CCIavg* by averaging the last *CCIAvgLength* bars of the *CCIvalue* calculation.

Finally, if the *CCIavg* is greater than 100, sell short the next bar at open. If *CCIavg* is less than -100, then buy the next bar at open.

ENTRY #36 – "BIG TAIL BARS"

General Concept

Tails in bars can sometimes suggest a trend is starting. For example, if a higher high is hit, and the bar shows a long tail on the down side, it suggests that lower prices were hit, rejected and then the bulls took control. If these "bull tail" bars outnumber the "bear tail" bars, and there are enough of them, it is a good time to enter long.

This entry takes advantage of bull and bear tails.

Tradestation Code

```
Var:BullBarTail(o),BearBarTail(o);
Var: Period(10); // lookback length for tail count
Var:thresh(5); //threshold for having a sufficient number of bull or
bear tails

BullBarTail = CountIF(Close>Open AND Open-Low > Close-Open AND
High > High[1], Period); // Bullbar with big tail
BearBarTail = CountIF(Close<Open AND High-Open > Open-Close
AND Low < Low[1] , Period); //Bearbar with big peak

If BullBarTail > BearBarTail and BullBarTail > thresh then buy next
bar at market;
If BullBarTail < BearBarTail and BearBarTail > thresh then sellshort
next bar at market;
```

Plain English Code

Look at the last *period* bars. For each bar calculate the number of bull tail bars and bear tail bars that occurred.

A Bull tail bar is when the close is greater than the open, AND the open – low is greater than the close – open AND the high is greater than the previous high.

A Bear tail bar is when the close is less than the open, AND the high - open is greater than the open - close AND the low is less than the previous low.

Finally, if the count of *BullBarTail* over the last *Period* bars is greater than the count of *BearBarTail* AND the number of *BullBarTail* is greater than *thresh*, then buy the next bar at market;

Or, if the count of *BullBarTail* over the last *Period* bars is less than the count of *BearBarTail* AND the number of *BearBarTail* is greater than *thresh*, then sell short the next bar at market;

ENTRY #37 – "NEW HIGH WITH CONSECUTIVE HIGHS"

General Concept

Anytime a market hits a new high, that it is a good sign for the tendency of the market to keep going up. This is really just momentum – a price moving in one direction tends to keep moving in that direction.

So, taken by itself, buying after the highest high is breached can be a good way to go. Turns out it is even better with some short term momentum confirmation with it.

This entry takes advantage of that. I have used it in currencies and metals. The reverse might work really well in stocks and stock indices.

Tradestation Code

```
Var:xbars(10);
Condition1= C > Highest(H,xbars)[1] AND C > C[1] AND C>C[3] AND C[1] > C[2];
Condition2= C < Lowest(L,xbars)[1] AND C < C[1] AND C<C[3] AND C[1] < C[2];
```

If Condition1 then buy next bar at market;
If Condition2 then sell short next bar at market;

Plain English Code

4 Conditions are needed for a long entry:

1. Close is greater than the highest high of the last *xbars*, calculated on the previous bar

2. Current close is greater than the previous close

3. Current close is greater than the close three bars ago

4. Previous close is greater than the close 2 bars ago

If all 4 conditions are met, enter a long trade at the open of the next bar.

4 of the opposite conditions are required for a short entry:

1. Close is less than the lowest of the last *xbars*, calculated on the previous bar

2. Current close is less than the previous close

3. Current close is less than the close three bars ago

4. Previous close is less than the close 2 bars ago

If all 4 conditions are met, enter a short trade at the open of the next bar.

ENTRY #38 – "START WITH AN AWESOME OSCILLATOR"

General Concept

As I have mentioned a few times in this book, I usually get my ideas, or at least the start of my ideas, from somewhere besides my brain. I try to build on and improve what others have created, and in that way make it my own.

Such is the case with this entry, which is based on the Awesome Oscillator by Bill Williams. I do not use it quite the way he does, but I have found times when it is effective.

This entry is still fairly simple, but also can be varied in numerous ways. One idea, that I have never tested, is to have an awesome oscillator calculation for the high, and another for the low. Perhaps they may converge and diverge, and that might lead to some interesting results.

Tradestation Code

```
vars: aback(1),bback(1); // Awesome oscillator lengths
vars: v1(5),v3(2); //average lengths
Vars: fatr(.5); //threshold for stochastic length
Vars: AO(0);
Vars:Price(0);

Price=(H+L)/2.;
Value1=average((H+L)/2,v1);
Value2=average((H+L)/2,v1+v3);
AO = (value1-value2);
//Bullish divergence
Condition1=AO[aback]>AO[bback];

//bearish divergence
Condition2=AO[aback]<AO[bback];

condition3=low<low[1] and (close-low)/(high-low+.000001)>fatr;
```

condition4=high>high[1] and (close-low)/(high-low+.000001)<(1-fatr);

if condition1 and condition4 then sellshort next bar at market;
if condition2 and condition3 then buy next bar at market;

Plain English Code

Calculate value1, which is the average of (high + low)/2 over last *v1* bars.

Calculate value2, which is the average of (high + low)/2 over last *v1+v3* bars.

Calculate *AO* = value1 − value2

Condition1 is true if *AO* of *aback* bars is greater than AO of *bback* bars

Condition2 is true if *AO* of *aback* bars is less than AO of *bback* bars

Condition3 is true if both parts below are true:
1. Current low less than previous low
2. (close–low)/(high–low) is greater than *fatr*

Condition4 is true if both parts below are true:
1. Current high greater than previous high
2. (close–low)/(high–low) is less than 1-*fatr*

Then, if Condition1 and Condition4 are both true, sell short the next bar at market;

Conversely, if Condition2 and Condition3 are both true, buy the next bar at market;

ENTRY #39 – "SECOND VERSE, (ALMOST) SAME AS THE FIRST"

General Concept

If you have read this, you probably realize that I like using concepts again and again, maybe with slight variations or twists, and other times be combining them with other "standard" pieces.

I don't do this because I am lazy (well, maybe just a little lazy!), but primarily because once I find ideas that work, I also find they work in many other situations and instances. It makes creating many strategies a lot easier, once you find some common ideas that work well.

This entry uses a modified part of Entry #38 (which also shows up in other entries), along with hitting a high/low close (which also appears in various other entries here).

The big twist, and the reason I include it here, in the entry month restriction. From January to June, this strategy can ONLY go long. And from July to December, it can ONLY go short.

Such a restriction could work well for agricultural markets – I use it for Soybeans. There has been a seasonal historical trend for prices to rise in the first 6 months of the year, and fall in the latter half of the year.

Other markets may have other seasonal tendencies, so you might have to do some seasonal analysis to see.

Tradestation Code

```
Var:xbar(10);
Var:thresh(.5);


If month(date)<=6 and close=highest(close,xbar) and ((c-l)/(h-l))<thresh then buy next bar at market;
If month(date)>6 and close=lowest(close,xbar) and ((c-l)/(h-l))>(1-thresh) then sellshort next bar at market;
```

66

Plain English Code

If the current month is January thru June, you can only go long. If the current month is July thru December, you can only go short.

From January to June, 2 conditions are required for a long entry:
1. Current close must be the highest close of the last *xbar* period
2. (close-low)/(high-low) is less than *thresh*
If both conditions are true, enter long at the next open.

From July to December, 2 conditions are required for a short entry:
1. Current close must be the lowest close of the last *xbar* period
2. (close-low)/(high-low) is greater than 1-*thresh*
If both conditions are true, enter short at the next open.

ENTRY #40 – "IT'S ABOUT TIME!"

General Concept

In the previous entry, certain months were good for bull trades, and certain months were good for bear trades.

This entry is a modification of that idea, except it uses time of day instead of the month.

I developed this back in 2017-8 for Bitcoin futures, and the concept could be applied to practically any 24 hour market.

The idea is that certain times of the day are more like to be buying opportunities, and other times are better for selling. To figure this out for your desired market, you have to do some data analysis. Just be careful not to use all of your data – leave plenty of untouched data to verify your findings.

Note that this idea went to breakeven after a nice start in Bitcoin futures as measured by XBT tracking symbol (see the accompanying figure), but the concept and idea could well work in other markets.

Tradestation Code

```
Var:barsback (10);
Var:BullSignalTime(False), BearSignalTime(false);

If (time>300 and time[1]<=300) or (time>2130 and time[1]<=2130)
then Bullsignaltime=True;
If (time>900 and time[1]<=900) then Bearsignaltime=True;

if Bullsignaltime and close>close[barsback] then Buy next bar at close
limit;
if Bearsignaltime and close<close[barsback]   then sellshort next bar
at close limit;
```

Plain English Code

If the current time has just passed 300 or 2130 (for 24 hour clock), and the momentum is up, then you can go long.

If the current time has just passed 900 (for 24 hour clock), and the momentum is down, then you can go short.

At times you can go long, if the current close is less than the close barsback ago, then enter a buy limit order at the current close price.

At time you can go short, if the current close is greater than the close barsback ago, then enter a sell short limit order at the current close price.

Entry #40 with a stop loss (no longer a very good entry for this particular market!)

Equity Curve Line - @XBT 46 min.(12/10/17 18:30 - 04/17/19 12:30)

ENTRY #41 – "FILTERED ENTRY"

General Concept

This entry is pretty simple. It consists of two parts. The first part looks for the highest or lowest close. Then a filter is used, based on the average range of yesterday being lower than the average range of two days ago.

Tradestation Code

```
Var:barsback(25);
Var:filter(False);

filter  = (highd(1)-lowd(1))< (highd(2)-lowd(2));

If filter = True then begin
```

IF C = lowest(C, barsback) and filter = true then Sellshort next bar at market;

IF C = highest(C, barsback) and filter = true then buy next bar at market;

End;

Plain English Code

If yesterday's range is lower than the range two days ago, then a trade can be taken, long or short.

Assuming a trade can be taken, if the current close is equal to the lowest close of the last *barsback* bars, then enter a short trade at next market open.

If the current close is equal to the highest close of the last *barsback* bars, then enter a long trade at next market open.

EXIT #1 – "NO EXIT CAN STILL BE AN EXIT"

General Concept

Take a look at this pseudo code:

Buy next bar at a 50 bar high

Sell short next bar at a 50 bar low

Looks like a simple breakout entry, doesn't it? But take a second look, and you will see this is really an exit approach, too. It is hidden, but it is a simple stop and reverse exit, and every strategy entry has this built in.

I'll explain, in case it is not clear.

Pretend you are long, and a 50 bar low comes along. What do you do? First, you EXIT your long positions, and then you go short. Same thing with the next 50 bar high – you EXIT the short and then reverse and go long.

You might be saying (best said with a California surfer accent) "bruh, that is basic stuff, dude! I need a real exit!"

Well, I am here to tell you that "stop and reverse" is a real exit, and most people just dismiss it or overlook it, since it is part of the entry. But there is a HUGE difference in the performance of these two strategies:

//Strategy 1 - Standard Stop and Reverse
    Buy next bar at a 50 bar high
    Sell short next bar at a 50 bar low

//Strategy 2 – Entry only
    If currently flat, Buy next bar at a 50 bar high
    If currently flat, Sell short next bar at a 50 bar low

Note that the basic entries are the same, but strategy #2 has no exit, as it only enters the market when you are currently flat. This leads to totally different performance when compared to strategy #1.

Most trading software automatically assumes that if you get a signal to go long, you are going to close out your short position first, since it makes little sense to be long and short at the same time (meaning, you are flat).

So, try out this approach on your next strategy, where you use stop and reverse, and alternatively with the entry signals only being for entry. You will be surprised at how different the results can be.

Tradestation Code

```
Var: barsback(50); //bars in lookback period

//STOP AND REVERSE (Entry also acts as exit)
If close=highest(close,barsback) then buy next bar at market;
If close=lowest(close,barsback) then sellshort next bar at market;

//Entry Only (Entry does NOT also act as exit)
If marketposition=0 and close=highest(close,barsback) then buy next
bar at market;
If marketposition=0 and close=lowest(close,barsback) then sellshort
next bar at market;
```

Plain English Code

For a stop and reverse, buy the next bar if the close is the highest close of the last *barsback* number of bars. Vice versa for a short.

For entries to be for entry only, if the current market position of your strategy is flat, buy the next bar if the close is the highest close of the last *barsback* number of bars. Vice versa for a short. Note that you will definitely need to add exits to this strategy.

EXIT #2 – "START SIMPLE"

General Concept

Most traders think a stop loss and profit target are two essential parts of any trading strategy. Well, they aren't. There is no rule that says you have to have one or both of these in a strategy.

Stop losses are just market orders, but they are not triggered until a specified price is hit. Typically they can get you out of a catastrophic trade, but usually they hurt the overall performance of a strategy. Many people like them though for the peace of mind they deliver.

Profit Targets are limit orders, where your price has to be exceeded (usually) for you to be filled. They can be very useful at times, by possibly taking advantage of favorable price spikes. If you are a long term trend follower, profit targets will likely not help. You'll likely be exiting a trend early.

I have many systems with both of these, but I also have quite a few with neither of these. And I tend to have more strategies with just a stop loss, and no profit target. Those strategies, I hope, take advantage of the adage "cut your losses, and let your profits run."

There are many, many ways to set up your stop and profit target levels. You could use support and resistance, chart patterns, etc. For this exit, I'll just show you 4: a dollar based stop, an Average True Range stop, and 2 hybrids of both.

Method 1: Base the levels on a certain $ per contract gain or loss

Method 2: Base the levels on the recent average true range

Method 3: Base the levels on the average true range, with a specified maximum value. This is nice if volatility gets really small, leading to small stops and targets. In this case, you will want the maximum of the ATR calculation and the minimum stop/target, to ensure a floor on the value.

Method 4: Base the levels on the average true range, with a specified minimum value. This is nice if volatility gets really large, as it prevents unexpectedly large stops or targets. In this case, you will want the minimum of the ATR calculation and the maximum stop/target, to ensure a ceiling on the value.

Tradestation Code

```
Var: stopdollar(1000); //stop level in dollars
Var: targetdollar(1000); //target level in dollars
Var: stopATR(2); //stop level ATR multiplier
Var: targetATR(3); //target level ATR multiplier
Var: stopdollarmin(500); //minimum stop level in dollars
Var: profitdollarmin(800); //minimum profit level in dollars
Var: stopdollarmax(1500); //maximum stop level in dollars
Var: profitdollarmax(500); //maximum profit level in dollars
Var: imethod(1) ; //stop and profit method

If imethod =1 then begin
Setstopcontract;
Setstoploss(stopdollar);
Setprofittarget(targetdollar);
End;

If imethod =2 then begin
Setstopcontract;
Setstoploss(stopATR*AvgTrueRange(15)*BigPointValue);
Setprofittarget(targetATR*AvgTrueRange(15)*BigPointValue);
End;
```

If imethod =3 then begin
Setstopcontract;
Setstoploss(maxlist(stopdollarmin,
stopATR*AvgTrueRange(15)*BigPointValue));
Setprofittarget(maxlist(profitdollarmin,
targetATR*AvgTrueRange(15)*BigPointValue));
End;

If imethod =4 then begin
Setstopcontract;
Setstoploss(minlist(stopdollarmax,
stopATR*AvgTrueRange(15)*BigPointValue));
Setprofittarget(minlist(profitdollarmax,
targetATR*AvgTrueRange(15)*BigPointValue));
End;

Plain English Code

For method 1, use dollar based stops and profit targets.

For method 2, use stops and targets based on the recent average true range, multiplied by *stopATR* or *profitATR*. Just make sure to convert this value into proper units (points, dollar value, etc) that your platform requires.

For method 3, calculate using Method 2, but include a check to make sure the stop does not go below some minimum value for the stop or the profit target. This helps you avoid having very small values during low volatility times.

For method 4, calculate using Method 2, but include a check to make sure the stop does not go above the specified maximum value for the stop or the profit target. This helps you avoid having very large values during high volatility times.

EXIT #3 – "TIMED EXIT"

General Concept

I am going to reveal my absolute favorite exit. I like it because it performs very well, in a variety of markets and timeframes!

I stumbled across this exit years ago, and could not believe it worked so well. It simply exits a specified number of bars after entry. No muss, no fuss.

I tried tons of variations of this exit over the years, and have included a few here. But the simple one still works the best.

So, for years I used it, but I was embarrassed to really tell anyone about it. Then, a few years ago, I was chatting with my friend and fellow champion trader Andrea Unger, and I confessed my use of this "stupid" exit.

Guess what?

He told me he used it too, and found it useful. Nice!

Then, I read an interview with legendary trader John Henry. He said this was probably his favorite exit too. Double nice!!

So, here it is. I guess it works because every entry signal is valid for only so long. This exit gets you out before the entry signal is no longer valid.

Tradestation Code

```
Var: bse(10); //bars to exit after
Var: imethod(1) ; //exit method

If imethod =1 and BarsSinceEntry>= bse then begin
Sell next bar at market;
Buy to cover next bar at market;
End;

//exit after specified number of bars, ONLY if position is currently profitable
If imethod =2 and BarsSinceEntry>= bse and openpositionprofit>0 then begin
Sell next bar at market;
Buy to cover next bar at market;
End;
```

//exit after specified number of bars, ONLY if position is currently losing

If imethod =3 and BarsSinceEntry>= bse and openpositionprofit<0 then begin

    Sell next bar at market;

    Buy to cover next bar at market;

    End;

Plain English Code

For method 1, exit position *bse* bars after entry.

For method 2, exit position *bse* bars after entry only if the current position is showing a profit.

For method 3, exit position *bse* bars after entry only if the current position is showing a loss.

EXIT #4 – "TIMED EXIT, BY DATE/TIME"

General Concept

Instead of just exiting after a certain number of bars, maybe you want to exit at the start of a new month, or the start of a new day, or even at a certain time of day. Lots of variations possible here.

The exit in this example is designed for longer term trades. I use it in a Gold strategy, and it exits 2 times a year – at the start of a new year, and the beginning of July.

You can easily modify this for different months, days or times.

Tradestation Code

if   year(date)<>year(date[1])   or   (month(date)=7 and month(date[1])=6) then begin

       sell next bar at market;

buytocover next bar at market;
end;

Plain English Code

Exit either a long or short position if one of two conditions is true:

1. The current bar year is different than the year for the previous bar (end of December to beginning of January)

2. The current bar month is July, and the previous bar month is June (end of June to beginning of July)

EXIT #5 – "PERCENTILE EXIT"

General Concept

This exit is fairly straightforward, and I have used it in stocks and stock indices. It is pretty powerful, and gets you out when price is turning against you.

This exits looks at recent prices, and calculates where the current close is in relation to those recent prices. It signals an exit if the current close is in the lower percentiles (for long positions) or upper percentiles (for short positions).

I have coded the percentile threshold at 0.5 (50%), but that could obviously be changed to whatever suits you.

Tradestation Code

Var: barsback(5);

if close<Percentile(.50, Close, barsback) then Sell next bar at market ;
if close>Percentile(.50, Close, barsback) then BuyToCover next bar at market ;

Plain English Code

Take the closing prices for the last *barsback* bars.

If the current close, in relation to all recent closes, is below the 50th percentile, then sell to exit any long position at the next bar at market.

If the current close, in relation to all recent closes, is above the 50th percentile, then buy to cover to exit any short position at the next bar at market.

EXIT #6 – "GET OUT, WHILE THE GETTING IS GOOD"

General Concept

As everyone knows, markets do not go in a straight line. They go up and down, back and forth. Sometimes, price moves in your favor, with a few consecutive bars in your direction. When that happens, you know eventually the good streak will end, so this strategy gets out "while the getting is good."

Of course, you could modify this code to make it longer or shorter than the 3 bars I show here. I picked 3 because, assuming each close up or down is independent of the previous close, once you have 3 consecutive bars up/down, the chances of the 4th bar being in same direction is only about 6%. In other words, pretty small.

Note that the way I have written this allows for some of the consecutive closes to occur before you are in a trade. I did this on purpose, since the consecutive close idea applies regardless if you are in a trade or not.

Tradestation Code

if close>close[1] and close[1]>close[2] and close[2]>close[3] then sell next bar at market;

if close<close[1] and close[1]<close[2] and close[2]<close[3] then buytocover next bar at market;

Plain English Code

Exit long position after 3 consecutive up closes. Exit short position after 3 consecutive down closes.

EXIT #7 – "A REAL WORKING END OF DAY EXIT"

General Concept

Tradestation provides a nice keyword for end of day exits: *setexitonclose;*

Problem is it usually doesn't work in real time!

It works great with backtesting, but in real time, unless you have a custom time session set up, Tradestation's exit will be sent after the platform senses the market is closed. Then, when it sends that order, the exchange rejects the order, because the market is closed!

This exit is designed to fix that. Note that it only works on XX minute bars, not daily bars and probably not most exotic bars.

Before using this, make sure there is at least one bar after the exit time you specify, or else it will not work properly.

I use this on many intraday strategies, regardless of market.

Tradestation Code

//exit at TimeExit if you are still in the position

```
Var:TimeExit(1605); //4:05 PM chart time
if Time>=TimeExit then begin
    sell next bar at open;
    buy to cover next bar at open;
end;
```

Plain English Code

If time is equal to or greater than *TimeExit*, close out the current position, long or short.

EXIT #8 – "DON'T GIVE IT ALL BACK"

General Concept

Nobody likes giving away profit, right? But nobody consistently gets the maximum out of a trade, either. We almost always get out at a point other than the peak profit point.

Realizing these facts, the trick is to allow the some flexibility in the position. Give it room to breathe. But at the same time, don't let all the open profit disappear. This exit tries to do just that, using the recent average true range as the guide.

Tradestation Code

```
Var:xATR(3);//number of ATRs to trail max profit with

if          maxpositionprofit-openpositionprofit          >
xATR*avgtruerange(15)*BigPointValue then begin
    sell next bar at market;
    buytocover next bar at market;
end;
```

Plain English Code

Calculate the current open position profit (Tradestation keyword: openpositionprofit) and the maximum profit you've had while in the current position (Tradestation keyword: maxpositionprofit).

If the difference between maximum and current open profit is greater than *xATR* * 15 period Average True Range (converted to dollars per contract), exit the position.

EXIT #9 – "PROFIT PROTECTOR"

General Concept

This exit is similar to Exit #8, except that instead of an amount based on average true range, this exit protects a certain percentage of profit. This only makes sense when a certain profit level is reached, since at the beginning of any position the ratio of open to maximum profit is 0.

So, this exit has two variables to adjust, the profit threshold in dollars and the profit protection ratio.

Tradestation Code

```
//set ppfloor and ppratio to protect profit
Var: ppfloor(1000); //don't invoke exit until $1000 profit level is reached
Var:ppratio(.60); //profit keep ratio – keep 60% of maximum profit

If maxpositionprofit>=ppfloor then begin
If (openpositionprofit/maxpositionprofit)<ppratio then begin
        Sell next bar at market;
    Buy To Cover Next bar at market;
    End;
```

End;

Plain English Code

If the position maximum profit is greater than *ppfloor*, than continue to the next step.

If the current open position profit divided by the maximum position profit is less than *ppratio*, then exit the position at the open of the next bar;

EXIT #10 – "EXIT WHERE YOU LIKE"

General Concept

Most of the previous exits have been based on the position profit. Many times, though, you will know the price you want to exit with a loss or profit, regardless of how your position is doing. Examples would be support and resistance points, or maybe swing highs and lows.

This particular exit will trigger long exits at LongProfExit and LongLossExit, and short exits at ShortProfExit and ShortLossExit. I have used a simple 10 bar high/low for the profit target and 7 bar high/low for loss levels, but you could of course use any desired price point and method instead.

Tradestation Code

```
Var:                                    LongProfExit(0),
LongLossExit(0),ShortProfExit(0),ShortLossExit(0);

LongProfExit=highest(high,10);
LongLossExit=lowest(low,7);
ShortProfExit=lowest(low,10);
ShortLossExit=highest(high,7);
```

Sell next bar at LongProfExit limit;
Sell next bar at LongLossExit stop;
BuyToCover next bar at ShortProfExit limit;
BuyToCover next bar at ShortLossExit stop;

Plain English Code

Calculate the long and short exit points based on whatever method you choose. In this example, I use the highest high of the last 10 bars for the long profit exit, the 7 bar lowest low for the long loss exit, a 10 bar lowest low for the short profit exit and the 7 bar highest high for the short loss exit.

Then, exit profitable positions with limit orders, and losses with stop orders.

EXIT #11 – "TIERED EXIT"

General Concept

This exit uses the general idea of exit #9, except it has different levels of profit protection. As the maximum position profit increases, it feels good to keep more and more of that profit, percentage wise. This exit permits this.

Tradestation Code

//set ppfloor and ppratio values to protect profit

Var: ppfloor1(1000); //don't invoke exit 1 until $1000 profit level is reached

Var: ppfloor2(2000); //don't invoke exit 2 until $2000 profit level is reached

Var: ppfloor3(3000); //don't invoke exit 3 until $3000 profit level is reached

Var:ppratio(0); //depends on maxpositionprofit
Var:ppratio1(.60); //profit exit 1 keep ratio – keep 60% of maximum profit
Var:ppratio2(.75); //profit exit 2 keep ratio – keep 75% of maximum profit
Var:ppratio3(.90); //profit exit 3 keep ratio – keep 90% of maximum profit

If maxpositionprofit>=ppfloor1 then ppratio=ppratio1;
If maxpositionprofit>=ppfloor2 then ppratio=ppratio2;
If maxpositionprofit>=ppfloor3 then ppratio=ppratio3;

If maxpositionprofit>=ppfloor1 then begin
if (openpositionprofit/maxpositionprofit)<ppratio then begin
    Sell next bar at market;
Buy To Cover Next bar at market;
End;
End;

Plain English Code

If the position maximum profit is greater than *ppfloor1*, than continue to the next step.

Set the proper value of *ppratio*.

If the maximum position profit is greater than *ppfloor3*, then *ppratio=ppfloor3*.

If the maximum position profit is greater than *ppfloor2*, but less than *ppfloor3*, then *ppratio=ppfloor2*.

If the maximum position profit is greater than *ppfloor1*, but less than *ppfloor2*, then *ppratio=ppfloor1*.

Finally, if the current open position profit divided by the maximum position profit is less than *ppratio*, then exit the position at the open of the next bar.

BONUS ENTRY #1 – "THE ULTIMATE"

General Concept

This simple entry uses Larry William's Ultimate Oscillator. https://www.investopedia.com/terms/u/ultimateoscillator.asp

Nothing special here, just looking to enter on the highest or lowest recent value of the oscillator in the past xbars.

I have keep the default parameters selected by Larry, and I use the same lookback period for long and short trades.

As always, you can change any or all of the parameters here. But be careful, since the more things you optimize, the more likely you are to curvefit.

Tradestation Code

Var: xbars(10);

if UltimateOsc(7,14,28)= lowest(UltimateOsc(7,14,28),xbars) then buy next bar at market;
if UltimateOsc(7,14,28)= highest(UltimateOsc(7,14,28),xbars) then sellshort next bar at market;

Plain English Code

Calculate the Ultimate Oscillator using values of 7, 14 and 28 (default suggested by Larry Williams). If the current oscillator value hits a local high/low over the last *xbars*, enter short/long at the next market open.

BONUS ENTRY #2 – "DAY OF WEEK STRATEGY, WITH A TWIST"

General Concept

Here is a pretty straightforward day of week strategy. It buys on Friday open, stays long over the weekend, and goes short on Monday open.

The little twist here is that new trades are only taken if the strategy has not lost too much money over a specified period. This in effect turns off the strategy when it is performing poorly. Simple, yet effective.

You will want to include some exits beyond the inherent stop and reverse exits.

Tradestation Code

```
var:TotEquity(0);
Var:lookback(200);
Var: LossAmt(3000);

TotEquity = NetProfit + OpenPositionProfit;

If TotEquity-TotEquity[lookback]>-LossAmt then begin

If dayofweek(date)=4  then  buy next bar at open;

If dayofweek(date)=5  then sellshort next bar at open;
End;
```

Plain English Code

Calculate the current profit/loss from the strategy, including open positions. If the strategy has lost more than *LossAmt* dollars in the last *lookback* bars, then do not enter any new trades.

Assuming you can take trades, buy on the open of Fridays, and sell short on the open of Mondays.

You will want to include some exits in this strategy, unless you just want the simple stop and reverse of the entries.

SOME ODDS AND ENDS

Here are some tips that will help you develop good strategies.

1. Just Because It Is A Variable...

All the entries and exits usually have one or more variables. Of course, you could set it up so all of these variables are optimized. That is not necessarily a good thing! In fact, it is usually the wrong thing to do.

Optimization is useful at times, but it is not the solution to coming up with a good strategy. It creates a better backtest, sure, but that does not mean the strategy will work better in real time. My experience is the opposite – the best optimized set of parameters usually underperform in real time, compared to sub-optimal parameters.

So be careful with optimization.

2. Intraday or Overnight?

Most of these entries and exits can be used as is for intraday trading (where you exit before the market close) and overnight trading (where you may hold on to trades for days or weeks at a time). Some of the entries/exits will require modification though.

Make sure you review some charts with the strategy active to make sure it is behaving correctly for intraday or overnight. Do that before you perform your major testing.

By the way, my experience is that overnight systems are easier to develop than intraday systems. But, I like the idea of intraday – being out and having no overnight risk – a lot more. Unfortunately, sometimes you have to take what the market gives you, not what you want.

3. Entry Symmetry

You will notice almost all the entries and exits I have shown are all symmetric – short trades are basically the mirror image of long trades. I did this intentionally.

For most markets, you do not want to restrict the ability to go long or short. Going long should be just as easy as going short. This is because most markets historically have gone up and down with near equal frequency.

An exception to this is the stock market. With stocks, there is an upward bias, so sometimes I will bias my strategies to favor long trades.

Note I also don't try to bias exits, even though many markets seem to "crash" faster than they rise.

I try to keep this symmetry really to limit curvefitting. I'm sure if I had separate long parameters and short parameters for each strategy, I'd get much better backtest results. But again, creating a great backtest is not the goal.

So, think hard about having separate parameters for long and short trades. You might find that doubling the number of parameters you test works well in backtest, but not in real time trading.

4. Order Types

I primarily use market orders in my trading. When all the pieces of my strategy signal "buy," I don't want to miss that trade. I just want to take it immediately. Of course, I realize there is a transaction cost to doing so, in the form of slippage.

The same slippage holds true for stop orders. Many people think stop orders protect them, but that is not always the case. Stops can have slippage, too. Sometimes, that slippage is extreme.

One order I try to avoid is limit orders. I like the idea of limit orders because they have no slippage, but too many times price touches my limit order, I do not get filled, and then the market takes off without me. That is frustrating! Also, limit orders get tricky when you trade multiple contracts and have a partial fill. So, be careful with limit orders. You might find trying to save slippage costs is more trouble than it is worth.

5. Entry/Exit Interaction Is Important

One important thing to remember is that entries and exits together make the strategies, not just one or the other. I have found entries that work great with one particular exit, but with other exits the strategy falls apart. And vice versa.

So, the interaction of the entries and exits is very important. This is crucial to remember while testing – don't discard an entry just because your first test with one exit is terrible. Try some other exits, too. Maybe you'll find something good with the entry when paired with a different exit.

6. Some Recommended Books & Magazines For Strategy Ideas

Here are some good books and magazines to get strategy entry and exit ideas. I still refer to these sources fairly often.

"Beating the FINANCIAL FUTURES MARKET: Combining Small Biases Into Powerful Money Making Strategies" (Wiley Trading) by Art Collins

"Profitability and Systematic Trading: A Quantitative Approach to Profitability, Risk, and Money Management" (Wiley Trading) by Michael Harris

"Beyond Technical Analysis: How to Develop and Implement a Winning Trading System" (Wiley Trading) by Tushar Chande

"Technical Analysis of Stocks and Commodities" Magazine

WHERE DO I GO FROM HERE?

At this point, your head might be swimming, and honestly I am not surprised. There is a lot of information here!

Here is how I recommend you proceed:

1. Learn Your Trading Platform

If you do not have a trading platform that you can test strategies with, I suggest you get one. Then, learn how to program strategies in it. I use Tradestation, as do most traders I associate with. I even have some special incentives with Tradestation for my students – just shoot me an e-mail for details.

So this is the first step – being able to program and run strategy performance tests.

2. Have a Structured Approach For Testing and Development

The proper test method is critical to success here. Many people just think they can just create a strategy, optimize everything, take the best overall result, and then trade it. If only!

The reality is proper strategy development and testing is a lot of work, and it is full of pitfalls. I developed my approach the hard way, by losing money in the markets. Eventually I developed a successful methodology. Here is what I use today to develop solid strategies:

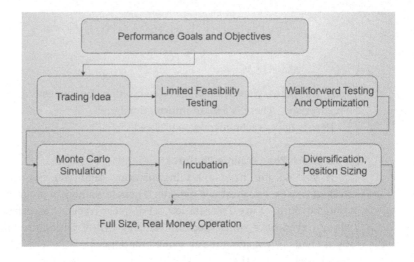

I call my method the Strategy Factory® approach. It works for me, and has worked for many others I have worked with.

Before you embark on testing entries and exits, make sure you have a solid approach to develop and test your strategies. THIS IS CRITICAL!

3. Select Some Markets, and Bar Sizes

I have some strategies that work great on many markets, and some strategies that work great only on one particular market. The problem is that I never know which is which until I test them!

So, before I start any testing, I usually lay out exactly what markets I am going to test, and what bar sizes I am going to test. Both of these are critical, because a strategy with Euro daily bars might perform totally different than a Japanese Yen strategy with daily bars, or even a Euro strategy with 120 minute bars.

4. Put Together Entries and Exits

This step is "create a strategy!" Take an entry I gave earlier, couple it with one or more exits I gave or exits of your own, and there you go – you have a strategy to test. Actually you have at least 2 strategies, since you can create a reverse of any strategy.

Just code the strategy, verify it and you'll be ready to test.

5. Start Evaluating

Use your test and development process you created in step 2 (you do have a process, right?!?) to establish what is a good strategy, and what is not. Then, get testing!

CONCLUSION

If you've made it this far, congratulations. But this signals just the start of your journey with this book. This book should be treated as a reference guide. Anytime you want to test a new entry or a new exit, just visit this book, grab an entry and START TESTING!

Good Luck, and please feel free to let me know how it goes.

Finally, I would appreciate it if you could take a minute or two to review this book on Amazon. THANKS!

DON'T FORGET THE BONUS MATERIAL

Now that you've finished this book on trading strategy entries and exits, I have some nice book reader bonuses for you. Simply go to http://www.AOKbooks.com/52book to get these bonuses:

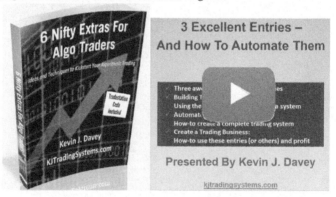

· **All entries and exits discussed in the book**, in Tradestation format as ELD files, ready to import.

· **44 minute video "3 Excellent Entries"** – advanced entry techniques, not discussed here

- **"9 Terrific Trading Entries, 7 Sensible Exits"** free e-book – new entries/exits not in this book
- **Invitations to free trading webinars** I regularly put on, and podcasts where I discuss trading
- **Advance notice of new articles and books** that I write
- **"6 Nifty Extras"** – not entries, not exits, but instead useful code snippets for Tradestation you can use

THANKS!

ABOUT THE AUTHOR – KEVIN J. DAVEY

As an award winning full time trader, and best-selling and award winning author, Kevin Davey has been an expert in the algorithmic trading world for several decades. Between 2005 and 2007, Kevin competed in the World Cup Championship of Futures Trading, where he finished first once and second twice, achieving returns in excess of 100% each year.

Kevin develops, analyzes, and tests trading strategies in every futures market from the e-mini S&P to crude oil to corn to cocoa. He currently trades full time with his personal account. He also helps small groups of traders significantly increase their trading prowess via his award winning algorithmic trading course, "Strategy Factory®." Kevin's Strategy Factory Workshop was awarded 2016 "Trading Course of The Year" by a prestigious trading website. More information is available at https://www.kjtradingsystems.com .

Kevin also helps educate the trading community via his best selling winning book, "Building Winning Algorithmic Trading Systems: A Trader's Journey From Data Mining to Monte Carlo Simulation to Live Trading," published by Wiley. This book was a 2 time winner of TraderPlanet.com's "Trading Book of The Year" in 2014 and 2016.

Kevin is a Summa Cum Laude graduate of The University of Michigan, with a B.S.E in aerospace engineering. Kevin also has an MBA with Technology Management Concentration from Case Western Reserve University – Weatherhead School of

Management, where he received the Dean's Academic Achievement Award with a perfect 4.0 grade point average.

Prior to trading full time, Kevin was Vice President of Quality and Engineering for an aerospace company that designed and manufactured flight critical components, managing over 100 engineers and support staff. For his efforts, he was honored with the prestigious "40 Under 40" Award from Crain's Cleveland Business Magazine.

Kevin currently lives outside of Cleveland, Ohio with his wife and three children.

OTHER BOOKS BY KEVIN J. DAVEY

For Beginning Algo Traders:

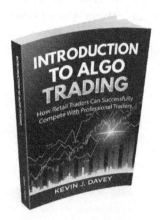

For Intermediate/Advanced Algo Traders:

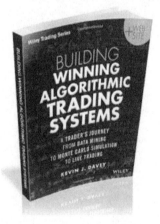

Both of these highly ranked books are available at Amazon.com. Click on either book above to be directed to Amazon.

Made in United States
North Haven, CT
08 April 2024

51065730R00057